Betty's Best

Betty's Best

A Cook's Family Cookbook

L. E. HEWITT

PUREWAL PUBLISHING, LLC
NOBLESVILLE

Published by
Purewal Publishing, LLC
176 W. Logan Street #105
Noblesville, Indiana 46060-1437

All rights reserved. No part of this publication may be reproduced, stored in a retrieval system or transmitted, in any form, or by any means, electronic, mechanical, recorded, photocopied, or otherwise, without the prior written permission of both the copyright owner and the above publisher of this book, except by a reviewer who may quote brief passages in a review.

All rights reserved.

Copyright © 2018 by L. E. Hewitt – www.lehewitt.com

Cover design by Joseph S. Anderson – TheForgottenArtist.com

Cool Whip, Kool-Aid, and Velveeta are registered trademarks of Kraft Food Group Brands LLC; Oreo and Ritz are registered trademarks of Nabisco/Mondelēz International, Inc.; 7UP is a registered trademark of Dr. Pepper/Seven-UP, Inc.; Rice Krispies is a registered trademark of Kellogg Company; Royal is a registered trademark of Clabber Girl Corporation; Karo is a registered trademark of ACH Food Companies, Inc.; and Jiffy is a registered trademark of Chelsea Milling Company.

ISBN: 978-1-7322880-0-3 (print version)
ISBN: 978-1-7322880-1-0 (e-book version)

Library of Congress Card Catalog Number: 2018942557

Printed in the United States of America.

Additional Titles by L. E. Hewitt

Life Between the Raindrops
My Wonderful Chaos
Chasing the Silver Lining
I Don't Have a Button For That
My Bucket List Has A Hole In It
Free TP and Frog Cures
Finally! An Unexpected Love Story

To August, Bessie, Lulu, and John

*For giving me Betty and Fred,
The best parents a kid could have imagined*

Contents

Preface	xv
Pizza	1
Cream Cheese Cookies	3
Apple Crisp	5
Grandma's Sugar Cookies	6
Punch	8
The Cake Lady	9
Betty Rolls	11
Zucchini Bread	12
Sour Cream Coffee Cake	14
Green Pistachio Cake	16
Zucchini Cake	18
Her Strength and Perseverance	19
Blackberry Cake	20
Cobbler	22
Pumpkin Bars	23
Cheesecake Brownies	25
Cherry Dessert	26
Dessert Salad	28
First Impressions	29

Blossoms	30
Chocolate Chip Cookies	32
No Bake Peanut Butter Squares	33
Soft Brown Sugar Cookies	35
Pumpkin Chocolate Chip Cookies	37
Joy in the Kitchen	38
Chocolate Chip Peanut Butter Cookies	39
Quick and Easy Peanut Butter Cookies	41
Tater Chip Cookies (My Personal Favorite)	42
Date Cookies	44
Butterscotch Chip Cookies	45
Old-Fashioned Soft Cookies	47
Waste Not, Want Not	48
No Bake Cookies	50
Frosted Ginger Cookies	52
Orange Cookies	54
Pumpkin Cookies	56
Cheesecake Cookies	57
Betty's Best Cutout Cookies	59
It's a Piece of Cake	60
Chocolate Fudge Thumbprint Cookies	61
Betty's Famous Pie Crust	63
Greene County Meringue	65
Strawberry Rhubarb Pie	67
Rhubarb Custard Pie	68
Pineapple Cream Pie	70

A Hearty Country Feast	71
Peanut Butter Pie	73
Butterscotch Pie	75
Lemon Pie (A Personal Favorite)	76
Appleless Apple Pie	78
Yellow Tomato Butter	79
Broccoli Cheese Soup	81
Frugal Living	82
Wedding Soup	83
Cabbage Soup	85
Stuffed Pepper Soup	86
Lemon Delight	88
Gooey Icing (A Personal Favorite)	90
Meatballs	91
Sharing the Love	92
Biscuits	93
Wilted Lettuce	95
Pineapple Banana Dessert (A Favorite)	96
Homemade Noodles	98
Nut Rolls	100
Nut Rolls #2	102
Miniature Nut Rolls	104
Betty's Love for Animals	106
Melt-A-Way Filling For Candy	107
Date Nut Bars	108
Bread and Butter Pickles	110

Country Sausage (A Favorite)	111
Banana Nut Bread	113
Homegrown is Best	114
Cranberry Salad	115
Cranberry Salad #2	116
Peach or Apricot Dream Salad	118
Barb Sauce BBQ	119
Potato Salad Dressing	121
Hot Peppers for Canning	122
Peppers and Tomatoes for Canning or Freezing	124
Cabbage Rolls	125
A Match Made in Heaven	126
Dumplings	127
Baked Corn	129
Rhubarb Jam	130
Peanut Butter Fudge	132
Peanut Butter Balls	133
Ham Loaf	135
Fred's Simple Hearty Recipes	136
Bacon Gravy	137
Fred's Cornbread	138
Hewitt Tater Soup	140
Coffee Toast	141
Tater Cakes	142
Buttered Tater Hash	143

Family, Food, and Lasting Memories	144
About the Author	145
Contact the Author	147

Preface

Some books are just ordinary books. Others become treasured old friends. I hope this one eventually falls into the latter category for you.

This book tells the story of Betty, through her food, mixed in with a few good tidbits from her ninety years of life.

Feeding people was her way of showing love, and she was darn good at it. She was well-known in her part of the world for her cooking and baking.

Her homemade pizzas, elaborate and delicious wedding cakes, handmade candies, and traditional country comfort food were enjoyed by just about anyone who ever knew her.

When you showed up for a visit at her house, you needed to be fed. If she attended any sort of community function, those folks also needed to be fed, and she was usually deeply involved in making that happen.

For me, she was Mom. She kept me well-fed too. For that, I was extremely grateful.

We raised most of what we ate. We had cattle, occasionally pigs and chickens, and vegetable gardens too. We picked apples, cherries, pears, peaches, plums, raspberries, strawberries, blackberries, grapes and more.

We canned and froze food every summer and enjoyed the

fruits, vegetables, and meats of our labor throughout the winters.

Mom was also the head cook at the local elementary school and the only cake decorator in the whole area. If you lived within twenty miles, there was an excellent chance that she made your birthday cake at some point.

I was quite lucky. My brother and I grew up with two very good cooks in the family. My mother and father both spent significant time in the kitchen, often together. The ingredients weren't fancy. The recipes weren't difficult. But, the results were amazing.

As my mother aged, she realized that many of these family favorites were stored nowhere but in her brain.

Sure, my brother and I learned to recreate some of these recipes, but she knew that unless she took action, many of these treasures would be lost forever.

In her mid-eighties, she tapped her memory and wrote down the best of the best into a composition notebook. This was not a simple task. You see, for her, cooking was as much of an art form as a science. Measurements were done by sight or taste. She worked at converting these intuitions into measurements that the average person could follow. She did not always succeed.

Therefore, there will be times in this book where you may need to use your own intuition to modify the ingredient amounts. I attempted to clarify and interpret her words to the best of my ability. But to eliminate all of them would have been as if I were eliminating a part of her. I want you to use your own common sense in those circumstances, just as she would have done. In that spirit, I have left ample room for you to write notes as you tweak the recipes and make them your very own.

I hope that these recipes will inspire your own creations that you will enter on the blank pages throughout the book. And I would be honored if this cookbook became your family's cookbook that would be passed down to future generations.

Creating this book has been quite nostalgic for me. It gave me the opportunity to revisit some of the best memories of things that made me who I am today.

I hope you enjoy the journey through these wonderful pages and find yourself sharing the love with your own family along the way.

Pizza

Crust

2 cups milk, scalded (let stand until lukewarm)

Add:
½ cup butter
3 packages of dry yeast

Let stand 10 minutes.

Add:
6 cups flour
2 tsp salt

Mix well either with a dough hook or by hand. Knead well. This will be enough for two medium baking sheets.

Sauce

6 oz tomato paste
6 oz water
1 tbsp brown sugar
1½ tsp Worcestershire sauce
2 tsp garlic salt
1 tsp oregano

Mix well.

Generously spread sauce on crust dough. Add whatever toppings you desire.

Preheat oven to 375 degrees. Bake until cheese is melted and crust is golden brown.

Cream Cheese Cookies

3½ cups flour
2 tsp baking powder
½ tsp salt
⅔ cup oleo
3 oz cream cheese
½ cup sour cream
1⅓ cups granulated sugar

Beat well.

Add:
2 egg yolks
1 tsp vanilla

Beat until fluffy. Chill in refrigerator.

Roll ¼" thick.

Bake at 350 degrees until browned.

Frosting

3 oz cream cheese
¼ cup + 1 tbsp oleo
2 cups powdered sugar

Beat well.

Cookies may be iced while warm or cool.

Apple Crisp

3 cups sliced apples
1 tbsp flour
1 tbsp water
¼ cup granulated sugar
½ tsp cinnamon
⅛ tsp salt

Mix above ingredients and spread into 9" square pan.

Topping

½ cup rolled oats
¼ tsp salt
¼ cup margarine
¼ cup brown sugar

Mix together. Then sprinkle over apple mixture.

Bake at 375 degrees for 35 minutes.

Grandma's Sugar Cookies

4 cups all-purpose flour
1 tsp cream of tartar
1 tsp baking soda
½ tsp salt
1 cup butter softened
1 cup brown sugar
1½ cups granulated sugar
1 cup canola oil
2 eggs
1 tsp vanilla extract

Sift together flour, baking soda, cream of tartar, and salt.

Combine butter, brown sugar, and 1 cup granulated sugar in a large bowl and beat with an electric mixer. Add oil, eggs, and vanilla. Gradually add flour mixture.

Chill dough 3 to 4 hours until firm.

Shape dough into walnut sized balls. Then roll in remaining granulated sugar.

Flatten balls on an ungreased baking sheet.

Bake in a 350 degree oven for 12 minutes or until lightly browned.

Punch

2 pkg cherry Kool-Aid
46 oz can pineapple juice
12 oz can frozen orange juice concentrate
16 oz 7UP soda

Mix Kool-Aid per package instructions.

Add juice and 7UP just before serving.

The Cake Lady

Betty was known as "The Cake Lady" in her rural Pennsylvania community. She had always been a noted cook and baker, but at about the age of fifty, she decided to go take a cake decorating class "for the fun of it."

Well, there were no bakeries within many, many miles of her rural community, and soon word got around. It started as a birthday cake here and there. Before she knew it, she was baking elaborate wedding cakes for just about every marriage in a twenty-five-mile radius.

As her teenage son, I helped deliver and assemble many of these masterpieces. Let me tell you, delivering a wedding cake down bumpy country roads with no air conditioning, in ninety degree weather, created some unique challenges.

Fortunately, my father became an expert at cake infrastructure, using such things as dowel rods to provide stability during assembly.

We all weren't experts when this started, but we certainly became experts over time.

Nobody in our poor, rural area had air conditioning back then. That made this whole cake baking business brutal in the middle of summer. I mean, who wants to turn on the oven when it's already ninety degrees in the kitchen?

Mom frequently iced these cakes with the fan blowing full

blast, wearing nothing but a pair of shorts and a bra. It was sometimes a bit of a shock to any unexpected guest who appeared on our back porch on a hot summer day. Mom would just tell them to come on in and to hang on for a minute while she went and found a shirt.

Betty Rolls

1½ cups milk (scalded)
½ cup sugar
2 tsp salt
¼ cup shortening
1 egg
2 pkg dry yeast or 2 oz cake yeast
¾ cups lukewarm water
5½ cups all-purpose flour, sifted

Stir sugar, salt, and shortening into scalded milk. Cool to lukewarm. Add 2 cups flour to milk mixture and beat well.

In a separate bowl, combine yeast and lukewarm water to dissolve. Add dissolved yeast and egg to milk mixture and mix well. Add remaining flour to mixture.

Once thoroughly mixed, turn out dough onto floured surface and knead until smooth. Place in large greased bowl and allow to rise until doubled in size.

Pinch and shape into rolls onto baking pan and allow to double in size again.

Bake at 350 degrees about 20 minutes or until desired golden brown.

Zucchini Bread

4 eggs
2 cups sugar
1 cup vegetable oil
3½ cups flour
1½ tsp baking powder
1½ tsp salt
1 tsp cinnamon
¾ tsp baking soda
2 cups grated zucchini (don't peel)
1 cup raisins
1 tsp vanilla
4 cups chopped nuts (walnuts, almonds, pecans, whatever you prefer)

Beat eggs, add sugar and oil.

In a separate bowl, combine dry ingredients. Then add to egg mixture. Add zucchini. Stir in nuts, raisins, and vanilla.

Grease and flour 2 loaf pans. Divide mixture into the two pans.

Bake at 350 degrees for 55 minutes on lowest oven rack. Allow bread to stand 10 minutes in pan before removing.

Sour Cream Coffee Cake

Topping

⅓ cup packed brown sugar
¼ cup granulated sugar
2 tsp cinnamon
½ cup chopped nuts

Combine topping and set aside.

Cake

½ cup softened butter
1 cup sugar
2 eggs
8 oz sour cream
1 tsp vanilla
2 cups flour
1 tsp baking powder
1 tsp baking soda
¼ tsp salt

For cake, cream butter and sugar in mixing bowl. Add eggs, sour cream, and vanilla. Mix well.

In a separate bowl, combine baking powder, flour, baking soda, and salt. Add to creamed mixture. Beat thoroughly with mixer.

Pour ½ of batter into a greased 9×13 pan. Sprinkle half of the topping mixture on batter in pan. Add remaining batter and then add remaining topping.

Bake at 325 degrees for 40 minutes or until an inserted toothpick comes out clean.

Green Pistachio Cake

4 eggs, beaten 5 minutes at medium speed
¾ cup water
⅓ cup oil
1 yellow cake mix
1 pkg Royal instant pistachio pudding mix
½ cup pistachios and walnuts mixed
¼ cup sugar
¾ tsp cinnamon

Combine all ingredients into a batter.

Bake at 350 degrees for 50 minutes.

Zucchini Cake

2½ cups flour
2 cups sugar
1½ tsp cinnamon
1 tsp salt
½ tsp baking soda
½ tsp baking powder
1 cup vegetable oil
4 eggs
2 cups shredded or grated zucchini
2 cups chopped walnuts

Mix thoroughly into a batter.

Bake at 350 degrees for 35-40 minutes.

Frosting

3 oz cream cheese
¼ cup margarine
1 tbsp milk
1 tsp vanilla
2 cups powdered confectioners sugar

Beat all ingredients until smooth. Frost cake when cool.

Her Strength and Perseverance

Mom was a strong country woman. She believed that she could do anything if someone just showed her how.

Aside from her cooking and baking skills, she was also known for constantly being busy with either work or charitable causes. Mom never let her age deter her from doing anything she wanted to do. She worked for the United States Census every decade clear up into her eighties. She rode big amusement park rides with her grandchildren into her late seventies. She didn't give up farming beef cattle until she was eighty-five.

Oh, and she always told you exactly what she thought too, whether you wanted to hear it or not. She gave you the truth with the best of intentions. She didn't subscribe to the notion of sugar-coating her opinions. It was part of her strength and integrity.

Blackberry Cake

2 cups flour
2 eggs
1½ cups packed brown sugar
½ cup shortening
1 cup blackberries
1 cup soured milk (combine milk with 1 tbsp vinegar and let stand 10 minutes)
1 tsp cinnamon
1 tsp nutmeg
1 tsp cloves
1 tsp baking powder
1 tsp baking soda

Mix all ingredients, folding in berries last.

Bake at 350 degrees until toothpick comes out clean.

Cobbler

Line bottom of 9×13 baking pan with fruit (peaches, apples, blackberries, etc.)

Combine ¾ cup sugar with 2 tbsp flour, and pour mixture over fruit.

Next, blend the following ingredients into a dough:
1 cup flour
1½ tsp baking powder
¼ tsp salt
2 tbsp brown sugar
¼ cup shortening (softened)

In a separate bowl, combine:
¼ cup milk
1 beaten egg

Add this mixture to the dough, blending thoroughly, and then spoon over fruit in pan.

Bake at 350 degrees for 40-45 minutes.

Pumpkin Bars

1 small can pumpkin
1 cup oil
2 cups sugar
4 eggs
2 tsp baking powder
1 tsp baking soda
½ tsp salt
2 tsp cinnamon
2 cups flour

Mix all ingredients thoroughly.

Bake on sheet pan at 350 degrees until toothpick comes out clean.

Icing

3 oz cream cheese
1 tsp milk
1 tsp vanilla
2½ cups powdered sugar

Mix all ingredients thoroughly.

Ice when bars are cool.

Cheesecake Brownies

1 pkg German chocolate cake mix
1 egg beaten
½ cup margarine
1 cup chopped nuts

Mix above ingredients, and press into 9×13 pan.

Topping

16 oz cream cheese
1 cup sugar
2 eggs beaten
1 tsp vanilla

Combine topping ingredients. Beat until smooth. Spread topping over batter.

Bake at 350 degrees for 30-35 minutes.

Cherry Dessert

20 sheets graham crackers (crushed fine)
1 stick softened oleo
½ cup sugar
1 tbsp flour

Mix together above ingredients. Spread in pan as crust, saving some for topping.

Filling

2 cups confectioners sugar
8 oz cream cheese
1 tsp vanilla

Beat well. Spread into crust.

Next layer a can of pie cherries on top of the cheese mixture.

Sprinkle with remaining graham crumble and chill.

Dessert Salad

1 medium container whipped topping
2 cans crushed pineapple
2 cans pie cherries
2 cans sweetened condensed milk

Stir in all ingredients and chill.

First Impressions

I first met Betty during an Easter weekend visit with her granddaughter, my then-girlfriend, now wife, Sara. In the short time I knew her, Betty never made a small meal.

The first night we were there, she made a ham big enough to serve eight. There were three of us, mind you.

Already full from dinner, Betty suggested I have a piece of chocolate cake. It was, of course, delicious.

Over the course of the rest of the weekend, I'm pretty sure I ate the rest of the chocolate cake myself, at Betty's insistence. She never seemed to take "no" for an answer, when it came to food.

After staying with her for a couple days, Sara and I were so full, we were ready to skip breakfast one morning. This was unacceptable to Betty.

Sara and I came up with a plan. We offered to make breakfast and, thankfully, Betty agreed. Our plan came to fruition as we cooked breakfast for Betty only, giving us some relief from all the food, tasty though it was!

– A memory from Andrew, Betty's grandson-in-law

Blossoms

1¾ cups flour
1 tsp baking soda
½ tsp salt
1 egg
2 tbsp milk
½ cup shortening
½ cup peanut butter
½ cup granulated sugar (plus a little more for rolling)
½ cup packed brown sugar
1 tsp vanilla
Candy kisses

Cream shortening, peanut butter, granulated sugar, and brown sugar. Add egg, milk, and vanilla. Beat well. Add dry ingredients, mixing well.

Shape into balls the size of golf balls. Roll in granulated sugar. Place on ungreased cookie sheet.

Bake at 350 degrees for 8 minutes.

Remove from oven. Press a candy kiss into the center of each cookie. Return to oven for an additional 3-5 minutes.

Chocolate Chip Cookies

1 cup margarine
½ cup granulated sugar
½ cup packed brown sugar
2 eggs
1 tsp baking soda
1 tsp salt
1 tsp vanilla
2 cups flour
2 cups chocolate chips

Mix all ingredients well. Spoon onto ungreased baking sheet.

Bake at 375 degrees for 12-15 minutes.

No Bake Peanut Butter Squares

1 cup margarine (melted)
1¾ cups graham cracker crumbs
1 cup peanut butter
2½ cups powdered sugar
2 cups chocolate chips

Combine first four ingredients and mix until well blended.

Spread evenly into a 9×13 pan.

Melt chocolate chips. Spread over above mixture.

Cool in refrigerator and cut into squares.

Soft Brown Sugar Cookies

3 cups light brown sugar
1 cup shortening
4 eggs
14 tsp hot water
2 tsp baking soda in 7 tsp hot water
3 tsp lemon flavoring
2 tsp cream of tartar
2 tsp baking powder
5 cups flour (more or less) to make a soft dough

Mix all ingredients thoroughly. Chill in refrigerator one hour.

Roll out dough with rolling pin to about ¼" thickness.

Cut into circles or cookie cutter shapes.

Bake 6-8 minutes at 375 degrees.

Pumpkin Chocolate Chip Cookies

14½ oz canned pumpkin
2 eggs
2 cups sugar
1 cup vegetable oil
2 tsp milk
2 tsp vanilla
1 tsp salt
2 tsp baking soda
2 tsp cinnamon
12 oz chocolate chips
4 cups flour
4 tsp baking powder

Mix all ingredients well. Spoon onto ungreased baking sheet.

Bake at 375 degrees for 10-12 minutes.

Joy in the Kitchen

I have so many memories of Gram involving food. In typical grandma fashion, she had a knack for convincing you that you were hungry. Small midday snacks turned into three-course meals. Food was never wasted, and leftovers were stacked in the refrigerator, ready at a moment's notice.

Many times, while Gram stood in the kitchen or sat on a barstool at the counter, my grandfather, Fred, would play the fiddle.

He would always ask, "You wanna see Gram dance?"

Of course, I would say, "Yes," and he would begin to play a square dance tune.

Gram would simply smile at first, then she would begin to dance around the kitchen. It was not just a place for food. It was a place filled with love and joy.

- A memory from Brandon, Betty's grandson

Chocolate Chip Peanut Butter Cookies

1 cup oleo softened
1 cup creamy peanut butter
1 cup white sugar
1 cup packed brown sugar
2 eggs
2½ cups flour
1½ tsp baking soda
1 tsp baking powder
½ tsp salt
2 cups milk chocolate chips

Mix all ingredients thoroughly. Spoon onto ungreased baking sheet.

Bake at 375 degrees for 8-10 minutes.

Quick and Easy Peanut Butter Cookies

2 cups peanut butter
2 cups sugar
2 eggs
2 tsp baking soda

Mix all ingredients together. Form into balls.

Bake at 350 degrees for 10 minutes on greased cookie sheet.

Tater Chip Cookies (My Personal Favorite)

1 cup shortening
1 cup packed brown sugar
1 cup granulated sugar
2 eggs
2 cups flour
½ tsp salt
½ tsp baking soda
1 tsp vanilla
2 cups potato chips, slightly crushed
1 cup chopped nuts (my favorite is a mixture of cashews, pecans, and almonds)

Cream shortening and sugar. Then add eggs and vanilla. Beat well. Add flour, salt, and baking soda. Continue beating. Add chips and nuts.

Spoon onto ungreased cookie sheet.

Bake at 350 degrees for 12 minutes.

Date Cookies

1 egg well beaten
1 cup sugar
½ lb chopped dates

Combine above ingredients in saucepan and cook slowly until thickened.

Remove from heat and add:
2 cups Rice Krispies
½ cup chopped nuts

Cool then shape into balls or logs.

Dip in chopped nuts or coconut and enjoy.

Butterscotch Chip Cookies

2 eggs
1 cup sugar
¾ cup margarine
2½ cup graham cracker crumbs
½ cup nuts
½ cup coconut
2 cups mini marshmallows
6 oz butterscotch chips
2 tbsp peanut butter

Beat eggs, sugar, and margarine. Put mixture in pan and bring to a boil and boil 2 minutes. Cool partially.

Add next four ingredients. Mix thoroughly.

Press into 9×13 pan.

Melt butterscotch and peanut butter together. Pour mixture over top. Let cool and cut into squares.

Old-Fashioned Soft Cookies

This is also the dough for filled cookies* (cherries, raisins, chocolate, etc.)

5 cups flour
1 tsp baking soda
1 cup shortening
2 eggs
1 cup sour cream
2 tsp baking powder
½ tsp salt
2 cups sugar
1 tsp vanilla

Combine all ingredients and mix thoroughly.

Refrigerate until easy to handle.

Roll dough out to ¼" thick or thinner for filled cookies.

Cut out into circles or squares.

* If making filled cookies, place half of cutout cookies on sheet, then spoon filling on top. Next place second cutout over filling and press edges of cookies together.

Bake at 350 degrees approximately 8 minutes for plain and 10 minutes for filled.

Waste Not, Want Not

Mom was the head cook at the local elementary school for approximately thirty years. This was not a place where prefabricated meals were heated and served. This was a kitchen where six women prepared a home-cooked-style meal for five hundred children daily.

She and her fellow cooks were loved by literally thousands of children over the years. Made-from-scratch rolls, thick-crusted pizza, and all sorts of amazing things came out of that place. Some of my personal favorites were pigs in a blanket, Maggie burgers, beef stew, and gondola pizza boats.

So, what's a Maggie Burger? It was the invention of another cook in the school district named Maggie. Envision a Sloppy Joe. Except, it wasn't. It was closer to a hamburger gravy consistency on a bun. I'm not sure what was in them, but they sure were good!

Gondola pizza boats? Those were a sort of sweet Italian roll with a hollowed out middle, filled with a pizza burger type of mixture and baked beneath a topping of mozzarella cheese. What kid wouldn't like that?

Each day, Mom would bring home a bucket or two of what the children hadn't consumed and returned on their trays. There was literally nothing wrong with the food. Yet, it was trash since a child had carried it across the lunchroom.

These buckets were often used to make our dogs' dinners.

They were happy on cheeseburger day or creamed turkey-over-biscuit day. But one particular beagle was tickled to death on spaghetti day. He simply loved the stuff! Between the school treats and the meat scraps we received a few times a week from the local butcher shop, our cats and dogs ate like kings.

The cows got a treat all their own. There was an outlet store for a company that supplied bread and bakery products to grocery chains. It was in a town about thirty-five to forty miles from our farm. They would sell pallets of the stuff that was outdated for somewhere in the neighborhood of five dollars each. Mom would go there periodically and load up the station wagon to the roof with this stuff.

The cows ate it like it was going out of style. We would drive through the pastures tossing bread and buns out by the handfuls. Those were some fun times.

No Bake Cookies

2 cups oatmeal
½ cup milk
2 cups sugar
1 stick butter
½ cup peanut butter
1 tsp vanilla

Boil milk, butter, and sugar for 4 minutes.

Remove from heat and stir in oats, peanut butter, and vanilla. Stir well.

Drop spoonfuls onto waxed paper and let cool. You may also add nuts or coconut to the mixture if you like.

Frosted Ginger Cookies

1½ cups margarine
1 cup sugar
1 cup packed brown sugar
2 eggs
½ cup molasses
2 tsp vanilla
4½ cups flour
1 tbsp ginger
2 tsp baking soda
2 tsp cinnamon
½ tsp salt
½ tsp cloves

Mix all ingredients.

Bake on ungreased cookie sheet at 350 degrees for 12-15 minutes.

Frosting

½ cup packed brown sugar
2 cups confectioners sugar
2 tbsp oleo
¼ cup milk
½ tsp vanilla
Pinch of salt

Bring sugar and oleo to a boil for one minute, stirring

constantly. Add milk and cook for 3 minutes. Remove from heat and add vanilla and salt.

Ice cookies when cool.

Orange Cookies

2 cups sugar
1 cup oleo
2 eggs
1 tsp baking soda
1 tsp baking powder
4 cups flour
1 cup soured milk (combine milk with 1 tbsp vinegar and let stand 10 minutes)
1 tsp vanilla
1 cup orange juice or ¼ cup frozen concentrate

Mix and bake at 350 degrees approximately 10 minutes.

Frosting

1 lb powdered sugar
1 tbsp oleo
Add enough orange juice to make spreadable

Ice cookies while still warm.

Pumpkin Cookies

2 cups flour
½ tsp salt
1 tsp baking powder
1 tsp baking soda
1 tsp cinnamon
1 cup shortening
1 cup sugar
1 cup canned pumpkin
1 egg
1 tsp vanilla

Mix all and bake at 350 degrees for approximately 10 minutes.

Icing

3 tbsp margarine
½ cup milk
½ cup brown sugar

Bring to a boil for one minute, stirring constantly.

Remove from heat. Add 1 cup + 2 tbsp powdered sugar and ½ tsp vanilla.

Ice cookies while warm.

Cheesecake Cookies

½ cup packed brown sugar
1 cup flour
½ cup walnuts
⅓ cup melted butter

Combine and set aside 1 cup of above mixture for topping.

Bake remainder of above ingredients for 12 minutes at 350 degrees packed into a 8" square pan.

Next, combine:
8 oz cream cheese
¼ cup granulated sugar
1 egg
1 tbsp lemon juice
2 tbsp milk or cream
1 tsp vanilla

Beat these ingredients thoroughly and pour over baked crust. Sprinkle with topping mixture.

Bake at 350 degrees for 25 minutes.

Betty's Best Cutout Cookies

1 cup granulated sugar
1 cup packed brown sugar
1 cup shortening
2 eggs
1 cup milk
2 tsp baking powder
2 tsp baking soda dissolved in 2 tbsp warm water
1 tsp salt
2 tsp vanilla
5 – 5 ½ cups sifted flour

Combine all ingredients. Mix well.

Roll out on floured surface and use desired cookie cutters.

Bake at 350 degrees on ungreased baking sheet until firm.

It's a Piece of Cake

Mom cared deeply about doing the right thing. Once, I recall, she had baked a birthday cake for a cousin. When delivering it, she went to get out of the car and caught her foot in the seatbelt. She tripped, and the cake went flying—somersaulting upside down—into my cousin's yard.

She was so mad at herself that she rushed home, baked a replacement, decorated, and delivered it that same afternoon in time for the party.

Our family just learned to live with this whole cake business. During busy times, it was not uncommon to grab a door handle or pick up the telephone and get icing on your hand. We were in sugary goo up to our ears.

We were also always a bit puzzled when someone would come to visit and ask for a bowl of cake icing to eat. To me, that was akin to offering me boiled eggs the Wednesday after Easter. I'd simply seen and eaten way too much already.

Chocolate Fudge Thumbprint Cookies

1 cup margarine
¾ cup packed light brown sugar
1 tsp vanilla
⅓ cup light Karo syrup
1 egg
3 – 3 ½ cups flour
1 tsp salt
2 cups finely chopped walnuts

Filling

⅓ cup Karo syrup
1½ cups semi sweet chocolate chips

Melt filling mixture in microwave and set aside.

Mix all remaining ingredients except nuts and roll into balls. Roll balls in chopped nuts.

Place on ungreased baking pan 2 inches apart. Press firm indentation into center of each ball with thumb.

Using a pastry piping bag fill indentation with chocolate mixture.

Bake at 325 degrees for 10-12 minutes.

Betty's Famous Pie Crust

1 cup shortening
2 cups flour
1 tbsp sugar
1 tsp baking powder
1 tsp salt
1 tbsp vinegar
⅓ cup milk

Cut shortening into flour and baking powder. Add salt and sugar.

In a separate bowl, combine vinegar and milk, then add to flour mixture. Mix all ingredients well.

Bake per pie instructions. Makes 1 two-crust pie shell.

If making a prebaked crust, bake at 350 degrees until golden brown.

Greene County Meringue

3 tsp cornstarch
½ cup cold water

Combine and cook to thicken. Cool completely.

Beat 3 egg whites with 6 tbsp sugar. Add to cooked cornstarch.

Beat thoroughly until light and fluffy peaks are formed.

Strawberry Rhubarb Pie

3 cups diced rhubarb
1 cup sliced strawberries
1½ cups sugar
2 tbsp minute tapioca
1 tsp salt

Combine all ingredients and pour into pastry shell.

Bake at 350 degrees for approximately 50 minutes.

Rhubarb Custard Pie

3 eggs
3 tbsp evaporated milk
2 cups sugar
3 tbsp minute tapioca
4 cups diced rhubarb
2 tsp oleo
1 tsp vanilla

Mix all ingredients well. Pour into pastry shell.

Bake at 425 degrees for 15 minutes.

Then reduce heat to 350 degrees and continue baking another 30-40 minutes.

Pineapple Cream Pie

8 oz sour cream
6 oz vanilla instant pudding mix
1 can crushed pineapple

Beat thoroughly. Pour into graham cracker crust. Refrigerate until firm.

A Hearty Country Feast

My maternal grandmother passed away in her early sixties. However, my grandfather, Pap, lived another twenty-five years. He was an old-fashioned farmer and not much of a cook.

So, every day around 5:00 P.M., our family delivered him his dinner on a trillet (a three-way divided skillet) and in other various bowls and containers.

Like clockwork, Pap came in from the farm, sat down at the table, unwrapped the foil from his delivery and pronounced, "Jesus Christ, Woman! There's enough food here for ten men!"

Then, he proceeded to consume every last bit of the feast along with several slices of bread. His ritual was one bite of food, one bite of bread, one bite of food, one bite of bread ...

While he ate and the adults visited, I typically explored outside.

Pap had no indoor plumbing. There was an outhouse in the backyard and a hand-pumped well for water just a few feet away from the porch.

An apple tree resided near the blacktopped country road. I'm not an apple expert, but it grew a smallish apple that visibly resembled the Gala variety.

Now, along the back fence in the yard stood a plum tree. Mom used those to make cans of plum jelly, butter, or preserves.

Immediately to the left of that tree was probably my favorite shed in the whole wide world. That shed had been used for many years to smoke meats. It was forever laced with an aroma of country ham and bacon. It made your mouth water just to stand in there.

Now, beside the shed was where you might find me hanging out about mid-August. You see, that was the location of a deep purple grape arbor. I frequently camped out under those vines on a hot day and ate my weight in grapes. Yes, I often paid for it later in the outhouse or in the bathroom back home, but it was worth it!

Peanut Butter Pie

8 oz cream cheese
¾ cup confectioners sugar
½ cup crunchy peanut butter
2 tbsp milk
1 small container Cool Whip

Combine first four ingredients using mixer. Gently stir in Cool Whip.

Pour mixture into either a graham cracker or Oreo crust.

Chill in refrigerator 2-4 hours.

Butterscotch Pie

3 egg yolks (save whites for meringue*)
1 cup packed brown sugar
3½ tbsp cornstarch
2 cups milk
¼ tsp salt
3 tbsp butter
1 tsp vanilla

Beat egg yolks. Add sugar, cornstarch, milk, and salt. Cook mixture on stove until thickened.

Remove from heat. Add vanilla and butter and stir.

Place in prebaked pie crust and top with meringue*.

Bake at 350 degrees until meringue is golden brown.

* Meringue recipe is on page 65.

Lemon Pie (A Personal Favorite)

1¼ cups sugar
6 tbsp cornstarch
3 egg yolks (save whites for meringue*)
2 cups water
⅓ cup lemon juice
1 tbsp butter
1½ tsp lemon extract
2 tsp vinegar

Mix sugar, cornstarch, egg yolks, water, lemon juice, and lemon extract. Cook on stovetop until thickened. Remove from heat and add butter and vinegar.

Place in prebaked pie shell and top with meringue*.

Bake at 350 degrees until meringue is golden brown.

* Meringue recipe is on page 65.

Appleless Apple Pie

2 cups water
1½ cups sugar
2 tsp cream of tartar
24 Ritz crackers

Combine first three ingredients in pan. Bring to a boil.

Add Ritz crackers and boil 2 more minutes.

Allow mixture to cool then pour into unbaked pie crust. Sprinkle with cinnamon and dot with butter.

Then bake at 400 degrees until crust is golden brown.

Yellow Tomato Butter

2 lbs yellow tomatoes
2 lemons cut into slices (do not peel)
2 lbs granulated sugar

Combine ingredients. Boil slowly until mixture thickens and clears, about an hour.

Can then be canned or frozen for future use.

Broccoli Cheese Soup

6 cups water
6 cups milk
12 oz package of your favorite noodles
2 lbs Velveeta cheese
1 tbsp minced onion
2 chicken bouillon cubes
2 pkgs frozen or 1 bunch fresh broccoli
Salt and pepper to taste

Cook broccoli, onions, bouillon cubes, and noodles in water until tender. Then add milk and cheese and simmer until well blended.

Frugal Living

Mom loved making the most of a bargain. Growing up during the Great Depression made those who experienced it much more frugal.

Things like wearing bread bags on your feet, to keep them dry in inclement weather, was normal.

Empty glass jars or plastic containers were never discarded. They were given a second life as a cat food bowl. Sometimes they were filled with berries and frozen.

They were also used to store leftovers in the fridge. Countless times I opened a plastic butter tub only to find that it contained coleslaw, apple sauce, or green beans. Mom may have known what was in each container, but to the rest of us, it was more of a treasure hunt.

Wedding Soup

4 quarts water
Cooked chicken (cooked and diced, using broth for part of water)
½ cup diced carrots
½ cup diced celery
1 onion diced
2 cups spinach
½ lb acini di pepe pasta (cook separately and rinse)

Combine all ingredients and simmer.

Meatballs

1 lb hamburger
I cup bread crumbs
1 egg
½ tsp minced garlic
½ tsp minced onion
Salt and pepper to taste

Combine all ingredients together. Mix well.

Form this mixture into small balls. Brown in skillet.

Add meatballs to simmering mixture and allow to simmer for about an hour.

Cabbage Soup

1 lb ground beef
1 medium head of cabbage
4 cups water
1 quart tomatoes (stewed or chopped)
1 chopped onion
1 clove crushed garlic

In large pot, brown the ground beef. Then add remaining ingredients and simmer until cabbage is tender.

Stuffed Pepper Soup

2 lbs ground beef
2 quarts water
28 oz diced tomatoes
2 cups cooked long grain rice
2 cups diced green peppers
2 beef bouillon cubes
¼ cup brown sugar
2 tsp salt
1 tsp pepper

In large pot, brown and drain ground beef. Add remaining ingredients and simmer 30-40 minutes.

Lemon Delight

First layer

Mix:
1 cup flour
¾ cup chopped nuts
1 stick oleo or butter (melted)

Press mixture into 9×13 pan.

Bake at 350 degrees for 10-12 minutes.

Cool completely.

Second layer

Mix:
1 cup sugar
1 cup whipped topping
8 oz cream cheese

Spread mixture onto cooled nut mixture.

Third layer

2 small packages lemon pudding mixed per box directions and spread onto second layer.

Final layer

Finally top with whipped topping and sprinkle with nuts.

Gooey Icing (A Personal Favorite)

Combine:
1½ cups milk
3 tbsp cornstarch

Simmer on stove until thickened, set aside.

Combine:
1 cup sugar
½ cup vegetable shortening

Beat these two ingredients with mixer for 10 minutes.

Then add:
½ tsp vanilla
½ tsp salt

Blend well. Then add to milk and cornstarch mixture and beat until ooey gooey and delicious.

Meatballs

2 lbs ground beef
1¾ cups bread crumbs
1½ cloves crushed garlic
½ cup Parmesan cheese
3 eggs
Salt and pepper

Combine all ingredients. Form into balls.

Bake at 350 degrees. Times will vary according to size of meatballs.

Sharing the Love

During the holidays, Mom always made her rounds delivering cookies and candies and other baked goods to lonely shut-ins and the elderly all around the region. The smiles she brought to their faces were priceless.

Other times of the year, she visited some of these same people to deliver a pot roast, or homemade rolls, or a fresh berry pie. She seemed to keep mental notes of who liked what and provided those gifts of food when she could.

We also grew fairly large gardens to supply ourselves with vegetables through the winter. Mom spent hours upon hours canning the fruits of our labor. Fortunately, there were often extras to share. Life was not just about providing for our family, but about helping others as well.

Biscuits

2 cups flour
3 tsp baking powder
1 tsp salt
⅓ cup vegetable shortening
¾ cup milk

Mix together ingredients.

Roll out and fold dough 5-6 times to ½ to ¾ inch thickness. Cut into rounds.

Bake at 425 degrees 12-15 minutes.

Wilted Lettuce

1 tbsp sugar
1 tsp flour
⅓ cup water
1 tsp butter or meat drippings (bacon works well)
Pinch of salt and pepper

Boil mixture to thicken then add 2 tbsp cider vinegar.

Pour hot mixture over lettuce and serve.

Pineapple Banana Dessert (A Favorite)

(2) 3 oz packages lemon Jell-O mix
2 cups boiling water
2 cups 7UP
1 cup miniature marshmallows
2 large bananas
20 oz crushed pineapple

Dissolve Jell-O into boiling water. Add 7UP and chill mixture until partially set.

Drain pineapple but save juice.

Add pineapple, marshmallows, and bananas to Jell-O mixture and set in refrigerator until firm.

Topping

½ cup sugar
2 tbsp flour
1 egg (slightly beaten)
1 cup pineapple juice (you may add water if necessary to make it 1 cup)

Combine these four ingredients and cook until thickened.

Remove from heat and add:

2 tbsp butter

1 cup whipped cream

Mix well and spread over Jell-O mixture. Sprinkle with chopped nuts.

Return to refrigerator until ready to serve.

Homemade Noodles

2 eggs
1 tsp salt
1 tsp baking powder
⅔ cup milk
Enough flour to stiffen

Roll out to desired thickness on floured surface. Let stand 20 minutes.

Cut into desired sizes and allow to dry covered by cloth.

Cook in water or broth until tender.

Nut Rolls

Dough

4 cups flour
1 lb butter
2 tbsp powdered sugar
1 large cake yeast
3 egg yolks (save whites for egg wash)
1 cup sour cream

Mix flour, butter, and powdered sugar into a dough. Crumble yeast onto dough.

In a separate bowl, blend together egg yolks and sour cream. Pour over dough mixture, and let stand for one hour.

Next mix well and refrigerate overnight.

Remove from refrigerator, and roll out dough mixture on a surface covered in ½ cup flour and ½ cup sugar.

Filling

1 lb (4 cups) ground walnuts
1 cup evaporated milk
2 cups sugar
2 tbsp butter

Bring milk, sugar, and butter to a boil. Remove from heat and stir in nuts.

Spread filling mixture onto dough and then roll up. Brush outside with egg whites and sprinkle with sugar.

Bake at 350 degrees until nicely browned. Baking times will vary depending upon size of rolls.

This recipe makes four large rolls or more smaller rolls.

Nut Rolls #2

6 cups sifted flour
1 tsp salt
3 tbsp sugar
2 tbsp dry yeast
½ cup warm milk
½ lb butter
3 eggs beaten
1 cup evaporated milk

Dissolve yeast in warm milk. Set aside.

Combine flour, salt, and sugar in a bowl. Cut in butter to mixture.

Next add in eggs, evaporated milk, and yeast mixture. Knead until smooth.

Divide dough into four equal parts. Roll out each section into about a 15×8 rectangle.

Filling

¼ lb butter
1½ cups sugar
2 cups milk
2 lbs finely chopped walnuts

In a pot, bring butter, sugar, and milk to a boil. Remove from heat and add walnuts. Allow to cool.

Spread filling mixture onto dough rectangles and roll up lengthwise. Place rolls on greased cookie sheet. Allow to rise for one hour.

Bake at 350 degrees for 35-40 minutes.

Miniature Nut Rolls

8 oz cream cheese
2 sticks butter
2 cups flour

Mix well. Cover and refrigerate overnight.

Filling

1 lb walnuts (ground)
1½ cup sugar
½ cup milk

Roll out dough. Cut into fourths, fairly thin on floured surface.

Cut into 3-inch squares, spread with filling and roll corner to corner. Roll in sugar.

Bake on ungreased cookie sheet at 350 degrees for 10-12 minutes.

Betty's Love for Animals

One of Mom's greatest loves was her love for animals, all animals. She never turned away an animal in need. She would put out extra cat feed knowing that the raccoons and possoms would come in the night and eat their share.

She loved her cattle and an old horse that she adopted. She always had a dog or three around. Mom even fostered two possums who were orphaned as babies.

If you were in the car with her and she spotted a turtle crossing a road, she would stop immediately and order you out of the car to gather up that turtle so that we could deliver it to somewhere safer. Never mind your own life was now in danger due to an oncoming semi truck, your job, by God, was to save that turtle!

Melt-A-Way Filling For Candy

2 cups white chocolate baking discs
½ cup milk chocolate baking discs
1 cup peanut butter
2 tbsp shortening

Microwave 30 seconds at a time, stirring until smooth.

Paint candy molds with favorite chocolate. Allow chocolate to set. Then fill molds with above mixture.

Date Nut Bars

1 pint dates
1 quart water
1⅓ tsp baking soda
1 quart sugar
¼ cup butter
4 eggs
2 quarts flour
2 tsp salt
2 tsp vanilla
1 cup nuts

Combine dates and water and simmer until tender.

Stir in baking soda and allow to cool.

Add remaining ingredients and mix well.

Bake at 325 degrees for 1½ hours.

Bread and Butter Pickles

8 cups cucumbers, peeled and sliced
2 cups sliced onions
1 cup sliced peppers (mild, hot, or green – whatever you have or like)

Mix above ingredients with a small handful of salt. Let stand one hour then drain.

Add:
2 cups sugar
2 tsp celery seed
2 tsp turmeric
3 inch stick or 1 tsp ground cinnamon
2 cups vinegar

Cook 20 minutes.

If canning, put in jars and seal while hot.

Country Sausage (A Favorite)

1 gallon ground pork
2 heaping tbsp salt
2 tsp pepper
2 tbsp brown sugar
Sage to taste

Make into patties and cook.

* For canning, cook until medium well, and then put into cans for cold pack.

Banana Nut Bread

½ cup shortening
1½ cups sugar
2 eggs
3 crushed bananas
3 cups flour
1 tsp baking powder
1 tsp salt
1 tsp baking soda
½ cup soured milk (combine milk with 1 tsp vinegar and let stand 10 minutes)
½ cup nuts

Cream shortening, eggs, and sugar. Add bananas, baking powder, and salt.

Dissolve baking soda in soured milk.

Add flour and milk alternately to creamed mixture, ending with flour. Fold in nuts.

Makes 2 loaves.

Bake at 300 degrees for one hour.

A simple glaze made with powdered sugar, hot water, and vanilla goes well with this.

Homegrown is Best

Looking back, I guess my food experience was just different. Aside from all of the cakes and pies, we also had a freezer full of beef, since we raised our own.

Repeatedly, I protested, "Oh no, not steak again!"

Steaks and roasts were staple foods. We were much more excited to have turkey or ham.

However, I must admit that the hamburger from a pasture-raised cow you butcher and process yourself tastes totally different from the hamburger in grocery stores. I don't understand why, but it is just not the same. This is also true of pork chops. The store-bought ones never compare.

Cranberry Salad

3 oz package cherry Jell-O
1 cup water
1 can orange-cranberry relish
1 cup quartered grapes
1 can crushed pineapple
1 cup chopped nuts

Mix well and chill.

Cranberry Salad #2

2 cups cranberries
2 cups water
2½ cups sugar
1 orange
1 cup grapes, cut in halves
1 cup chopped celery
1 cup crushed pineapple
3 oz package cherry Jell-O

Simmer first three ingredients 10 minutes.

Remove from heat. Then add Jell-O and let thicken.

Add remaining ingredients and chill.

Peach or Apricot Dream Salad

6 oz of either peach or apricot Jell-O
2 cups boiling water
8 oz cream cheese
2 cups crushed pineapple
11 oz mandarin oranges
1 envelope powdered whipped topping mix
1 cup miniature marshmallows

Dissolve Jell-O in boiling water.

Beat cream cheese until fluffy, and then beat into hot Jell-O.

Add 1 cup pineapple. Chill until partially set.

Add remainder of fruits. Fold in whipped topping and marshmallows. Sprinkle with nuts. Chill.

Barb Sauce BBQ

1 tsp mustard
1 tsp Worcestershire sauce
3 tbsp cider vinegar
3 tsp brown sugar
¾ cup chili sauce
½ cup water

Mix well and simmer 10 minutes.

Potato Salad Dressing

1 cup cider vinegar
1 cup water
3 eggs
1 cup sugar
1 tsp dry mustard
1 tbsp flour
1 tbsp butter
½ tsp salt

Beat eggs. Add sugar, mustard, flour, butter, and salt. Beat until smooth.

Add vinegar and water. Simmer for 5 minutes.

Hot Peppers for Canning

2 qts vinegar
1 qt water
1 tsp salt

Heat to near boiling and pour over fresh whole peppers in canning jar. Seal and process.

Peppers and Tomatoes for Canning or Freezing

12 peppers sliced
6 cups tomatoes (scalded and peeled)
3 tbsp oil
3 tbsp salt

Cook down to desired thickness.

Then pour hot mixture into cans and seal. Or cool and then place in gallon freezer bags and seal.

Cabbage Rolls

1½ lbs ground beef
⅓ cup cooked rice
1 chopped green pepper
1 chopped onion
1 cup diced tomatoes
Salt and pepper to taste
15 oz tomato sauce
1 head cabbage

Boil cabbage head until pliable.

Mix all ingredients but tomato sauce. Stuff and roll cabbage leaves with mixture. Place in baking dish and pour over with tomato sauce.

Bake at 350 degrees for at least one hour.

A Match Made in Heaven

Betty and Fred shared a love story spanning many years of dating and fifty plus years of marriage. They also shared much quality time in the kitchen. Together they would spend a day making homemade vegetable soup or shelling, husking, and peeling their harvests from the garden.

There were some things that Dad made better than Mom, and he would never share his secrets with her when it came to cooking. My dad's cornbread and tater soup were two cases in point. They weren't fancy. None of his meals were. But, no matter how hard Mom tried, her version was just never quite as good as his.

This woman was known throughout the county for her cooking and baking, yet a man in her own house could outdo her at making this meal. Fortunately, she was a good sport about it.

If you're wondering, the proper way to eat this meal is to split your square of cornbread on a plate, and then ladle the tater soup over the cornbread. It's a match made in heaven, just like my parents.

Dumplings

1 egg
2 tbsp water
½ tsp salt
1½ tsp baking powder
Flour to stiffen into a thick batter

Combine all ingredients. Mix well. Add enough flour to stiffen to desired consistency.

Spoon-drop batter into a boiling broth or beans. Cover and simmer 20 minutes.

DO NOT PEEK!

Baked Corn

1 can creamed corn
1 can whole kernel corn
1 egg
½ box Jiffy corn muffin mix
4 oz sour cream
Salt and pepper to taste
½ stick butter

Mix all ingredients.

Bake in oven dish at 350 degrees for 45 minutes, stirring once.

Optional – Add shredded cheese on top for final 15 minutes of baking.

Rhubarb Jam

4 cups diced rhubarb
4 cups sugar
20 oz crushed pineapple
6 oz strawberry Jell-O mix

Bring rhubarb, sugar, and pineapple to a boil. Allow to boil gently for 2 minutes.

Add Jell-O mix and boil an additional minute.

If canning, pour hot mixture into jars and seal. Otherwise divide into containers and cool.

Peanut Butter Fudge

2 cups sugar
⅔ cup milk

Cook to soft boil.

Stir in:
1 cup peanut butter
1 cup marshmallow cream

Remove from heat and add:
1 tbsp butter
1 tsp vanilla

Pour mixture into greased pan and cut into squares when cool.

Peanut Butter Balls

1 box + 1 cup powdered sugar
12 oz peanut butter
2 sticks butter
½ tsp vanilla

Beat until smooth and roll into balls.

Dip into melted chocolate and place on waxed paper.

Ham Loaf

2½ lbs smoked ham (ground)
½ lb ground pork
I cup crushed saltine crackers
1 cup milk
½ cup chopped onion
2 eggs beaten
¼ tsp pepper

Mix thoroughly and place in loaf pan.

Bake at 350 degrees for 2 hours.

Glaze sauce

1 cup crushed pineapple
1 tbsp brown sugar
2 tsp Worcestershire sauce

Simmer these three ingredients until thickened. Pour over finished loaf slices.

Fred's Simple Hearty Recipes

My dad, Fred, was also a good cook in his own right. This book wouldn't be complete without a few Fred specialties included. The remainder of the recipes in this cookbook are Dad's creations. His recipes are of a much more informal nature. They are also some of my all-time favorites.

Bacon Gravy

Fry about a pound of bacon to a crispy state. Remove bacon from the grease and crumble. (Of course a few slices always go missing during this process.)

Mix 2 cups of milk with ½ cup flour to form a smooth mixture. Add to bacon grease and stir constantly over medium heat. Add additional milk or flour to reach desired consistency.

Add back in uneaten bacon crumbles.

Ladle over a slice of homemade bread and enjoy.

Fred's Cornbread

1 cup flour
1 cup yellow cornmeal
⅔ cup sugar
3 tsp baking powder
1 egg
1 cup milk
⅓ cup cooking oil

Mix well.

Bake at 400 degrees in 9-inch square pan for 20-25 minutes.

Hewitt Tater Soup

5 lbs potatoes, peeled and cut into 1-inch cubes
1 onion chopped
1 tsp celery seed
Salt and pepper to taste

Boil potatoes until tender enough to split with a fork. Just do not overcook them.

Drain potatoes, leaving an inch of water in the bottom of the stock pot. Add onion, celery seed, salt, and pepper.

Next add:
½ lb butter
6 cups milk

Finally add 2 tbsp cornstarch mixed with small amount of water to form a paste.

Simmer a few more minutes and enjoy.

This soup was always a favorite ladled over Dad's cornbread. (See cornbread recipe on previous page.)

Coffee Toast

1 slice of bread, darkly toasted
1 cup coffee or tea
2 tsp sugar

Break toast into 1-inch pieces. Place in cup and pour in coffee. Add sugar and eat with a spoon.

Tater Cakes

Save leftover mashed potatoes from dinner last night. Form into hamburger-size patties.

Heat oil or butter in a large skillet.

Place potato patties in heated skillet. Fry until golden brown and crispy on each side.

For a nifty kick, add some ramps to the potato mixture before frying.

Buttered Tater Hash

5 lbs potatoes, cut into 1-inch cubes and cooked until fork tender

Drain and then add:
1 stick butter
Salt and pepper to taste

Next eat some taters and save some for the next day.

The next day, throw remaining taters in hot skillet with butter or oil.

Add:
1 diced onion
½ diced green pepper
1 cup diced ham

Fry until taters are browning and onion is translucent.

Family, Food, and Lasting Memories

It is my hope that you will enjoy these stories and recipes with your own family and that this book may play a part in your lives for many generations to come.

Gatherings centered around these and other country comfort foods are often gatherings filled with love, family, sharing, and giving.

Treasure those times. For, just like my mother and father, they will be gone one day. But luckily, the wonderful memories remain and live on.

About the Author

Author L. E. Hewitt is a product of the rural Appalachian hills of southwestern Pennsylvania, where he was raised in a family filled with love, laughter, hayfields, music, tater gardens, cows, cats, pigs, dogs, horses, and possums. What more could a feller ask for?

As an adult, his musical dreams took L. E. to Tennessee where he was able to fulfill many dreams as a studio and road musician before finally settling down to raise a family and run a business.

By his mid-forties, he was chasing a new dream. Now, in his mid-fifties and eight books later, he is still bringing laughter and a positive outlook to his readers.

L. E. Hewitt loves to hear from his readers!

If you enjoyed this book, please leave a review online at Amazon, Barnes and Noble, or Goodreads!

Go online to like L. E. Hewitt's Facebook Page!

Check out the latest news and events on L. E. Hewitt's website: www.lehewitt.com

www.ingramcontent.com/pod-product-compliance
Lightning Source LLC
Chambersburg PA
CBHW071207070526
44584CB00019B/2944